# LET IT BEGIN HERE!

THE DAY THE AMERICAN REVOLUTION BEGAN

 Actual Times

VOLUME ONE      APRIL 19, 1775      $7.99

# LET IT BEGIN HERE!

## DON BROWN

ROARING BROOK PRESS

NEW YORK

*To Mindy and Lloyd*

Published by Flash Point, an imprint of Roaring Brook Press

Roaring Brook Press is a division of Holtzbrinck Publishing Holdings Limited Partnership

175 Fifth Avenue, New York, New York 10010

www.roaringbrookpress.com

Distributed in Canada by H. B. Fenn and Company Ltd.

Library of Congress Cataloging-in-Publication Data

Brown, Don, 1949-

Let it begin here! : April 19, 1775, the day the American Revolution began / Don Brown. – 1st ed.

p. cm.

HARDCOVER ISBN: 978-1-59643-221-5    PAPERBACK ISBN: 978-1-59643-645-9

1. Lexington, Battle of, Lexington, Mass., 1775–Juvenile literature. 2. Concord, Battle of, Concord, Mass.,

1775–Juvenile literature. I. Title.

E241.L6B77 2008    973.3'311–dc22    2008011221

Roaring Brook Press books are available for special promotions and premiums.

For details contact: Director of Special Markets, Holtzbrinck Publishers.

First edition December 2008

First paperback edition August 2010

Book design by Jennifer Browne

Printed in May 2010 in China by South China Printing Co. Ltd., Dongguan City, Guangdong Province

Hardcover: 4   6   8   10   9   7   5

Paperback: 2   4   6   8   10   9   7   5   3   1

*April 19, 1775*

A strong brown mare carried a messenger through a
moonlit night to a simple house on a country lane. The
messenger banged on the door. Windows flew open and,
like turtles emerging from their shells, sleepy heads popped out to
discover the source of the commotion.

It was vital news the messenger brought. News, it might be said,
that took twelve years to arrive.

In 1763, England's young King George III, only twenty-six years old, had found himself the victor of the Seven Years' War. Britain had defeated the French, Austrians, and Spanish and had won colonies around the world. Celebration was surely in order.

But George III could not celebrate.

Victory had not come cheap. Britain bowed under a huge war debt and the expense of governing an enlarged, far-flung empire. Something had to be done.

The king and his ministers cast about for a solution, and their eyes fell on Britain's American colonies. Convinced that the Americans were not contributing their fair share to the mother country, King George and his advisers decided to lighten the burden on the empire by lightening the pocketbooks of the Americans. New taxes — on cloth, sugar, almanacs, newspapers, and tea, to name a few — were levied on the American colonies.

Dismayed at first, the Americans soon grew angry, then riotous. Violence flared. Britain answered with harder, stricter laws. Warm feelings that had existed for generations between Britain and her American colonies chilled.

By 1775, both sides were prepared for war. The time for "conciliation, moderation, and reasoning is over. Nothing can be done but by forcible means," said General Thomas Gage, the British military commander in America.

It was tough talk, but the general, a sober-faced man used to making weighty decisions, was torn. America had been his home for nearly twenty years. He'd acquired property and wed a beautiful New Jersey heiress. "Bloody crisis" had to be avoided. But how?

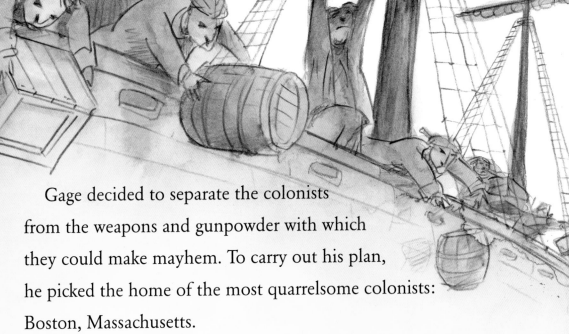

Gage decided to separate the colonists from the weapons and gunpowder with which they could make mayhem. To carry out his plan, he picked the home of the most quarrelsome colonists: Boston, Massachusetts.

General Gage thought the Bostonians to be the "greatest bullies." In 1773, Bostonians had dumped crates of tea in the harbor rather than pay tax on it. The Boston Tea Party cheered the Yankees, but left the king considerably less amused. He shut down the harbor, crippling business and punishing the Bostonians. But the king's attempt to enforce the obedience of his colonists backfired. Opposition to King George's rule drew the colonists together in opposition. In September 1774, representatives of the American colonies gathered for the First Continental Congress in Philadelphia.

Meanwhile, General Gage made his first move to disarm
the colonists. In the early hours of September 1, 1774, his troops
sneaked from their Boston barracks to a powder house in
nearby Middlesex County, the largest supply of gunpowder in
Massachusetts. There, they grabbed 250 half barrels and returned
home before the outfoxed colonists awakened to the seizure.

News of the powder "robbery" unleashed terrible anger and sent thousands of furious Yankees into the streets. The mob fell upon hated Tories, Americans who sympathized with the king, and threatened them, smashed their property, and chased them from their homes.

Afterward, silversmith Paul Revere and others opposing the king vowed not to be surprised again by General Gage. Revere, square jawed and steady eyed, organized a Committee of Observers, lookouts on watch for another powder raid by the "regulars," as the British soldiers were known.

On April 18, 1775, a spy brought news to Revere and his friends that Gage's soldiers were preparing to march again. Revere had already concocted a plan to spread the word.

He sent John Pulling and Robert Newman to the old North Church with two "lanthorns," lanterns fashioned with paper-thin slices of cow horn in place of glass. They climbed to the top of the church's steeple, lit the lanthorns, and held them out a window.

The twinkling lights were a message for Revere's allies outside of Boston.

"If the British were out by water we would show two lanthorns . . . and if by land, one."

The two lights sent news spreading throughout nearby towns: Beware — soldiers were coming quickly by boat!

Meanwhile, on the Boston waterfront, Colonel Francis Smith led nearly nine hundred British infantrymen, grenadiers, and royal marines onto longboats. They dutifully stood closely packed as sailors rowed them across the Back Bay to Cambridge. They waded ashore at a marshy beach, soaking themselves up to their waists. The night was cool and the men shivered inside their linen britches and red woolen coats.

Only their officers knew where they were going or what was expected of them. Each soldier carried a day's provisions and thirty-six rounds of powder and ball for their muskets.

At 2 a.m. they started forward, tramping one square-toed boot in front of the other.

On their heels was the determined Paul Revere. He feared the redcoats meant to march to Lexington and capture Samuel Adams and John Hancock, leaders of the colonial opposition who were staying at Minister Jonas Clarke's home there.

After a rowboat took Revere to Cambridge, he mounted a mare named Brown Beauty and raced off. The moon was bright. He rode hard for an hour, dodging British patrols, until he reached the Clarke house at midnight. Revere banged on the door.

Windows flew open and, like turtles emerging from their shells, sleepy heads popped out, including Adams's and Hancock's.

The men believed that Gage's main mission was to seize and destroy the colonists' gunpowder at Concord. Revere, accompanied by rider William Dawes, was sent on to Concord with a warning while Hancock and Adams made their escape from Minister Clarke's house.

As they left, the Lexington militia mustered. Fifty to seventy men raced to join John Parker, their captain and a veteran of the earlier French and Indian Wars. A farmer and mechanic, Parker was forty-six and dying of tuberculosis. His men ignored his ill health and unflinchingly followed him onto the grassy field at the town's center.

Dawn and the redcoats arrived together. At the head of their march was Major John Pitcairn, leading about 240 men.

"If I draw my sword but half out of its scabbard, the whole banditti of Massachusetts will run away," he once bragged.

Now, on the Lexington Green, two lines of the so-called banditti stood before him.

Captain Parker told his men, "Stand your ground! Don't fire unless fired upon! But if they want to have a war, let it begin here."

"Huzza! Huzza! Huzza!" yelled the regulars and formed a battle line.

Onlookers gathered at the edges of the green.

From horseback, Pitcairn shouted, "Throw down your arms, ye villains, ye rebels!"

Greatly outnumbered, Parker probably recognized the folly of resisting. He ordered his men to "disperse and not fire," and most of them turned away. None dropped their weapons.

A shot!

"Some of the rebels who had jumped over a wall fired," Pitcairn said.

"Some of the villains [who] got over the hedge fired at us," said another British officer.

It came from "the corner of a large house," other soldiers claimed.

Militiaman Thomas Fessenden said an officer next to Pitcairn "fired a pistol."

Minister Clarke also claimed one of Pitcairn's officers "fired a pistol towards the militia as they were dispersing."

Was it the British? The Yankees?

The answer remains a mystery.

But the shot acted as a signal to the regulars who, without orders, fired first in ragged single shots, then in combined, roaring volleys.

Their muskets spewed heavy leaden balls, belching so much smoke as they fired that clouds of it covered the green, hiding shooters and shot-at alike.

Balls clipped part of Lexington's Ebenezer Munroe's earlocks, scraped his clothes, and pierced his arm. Militiaman Robert Munroe fell dead where he stood.

Shot in the chest, Jonathan Harrington crawled to his house at the edge of the green and died on his own doorstep as his wife and son watched.

Jonas Parker, a kinsman of the captain, fell wounded. On the ground, he struggled to load his gun.

The Yankees fired back.

"All was confusion and distress," militiaman Joseph Seabrook said.

Bullets flew. Men fell. The redcoats charged with bayonets and killed Jonas Parker.

Colonel Smith arrived and discovered seven dead militiamen, one dead regular, others wounded, and his men acting less like soldiers than a mob. He forced them back into disciplined ranks, saying, "I was desirous of putting a stop to all further slaughter."

Smith allowed his men three victory cheers before ordering them to Concord. For most, it was the first time they learned of their mission.

They left the dead and the grieving of Lexington. But as the regulars marched the six miles to Concord, thousands of militiamen from surrounding towns rallied. The lanthorns Revere had shone hours earlier had set in motion alarm riders, signal shots, and beacon fires that had spread the call to arms everywhere.

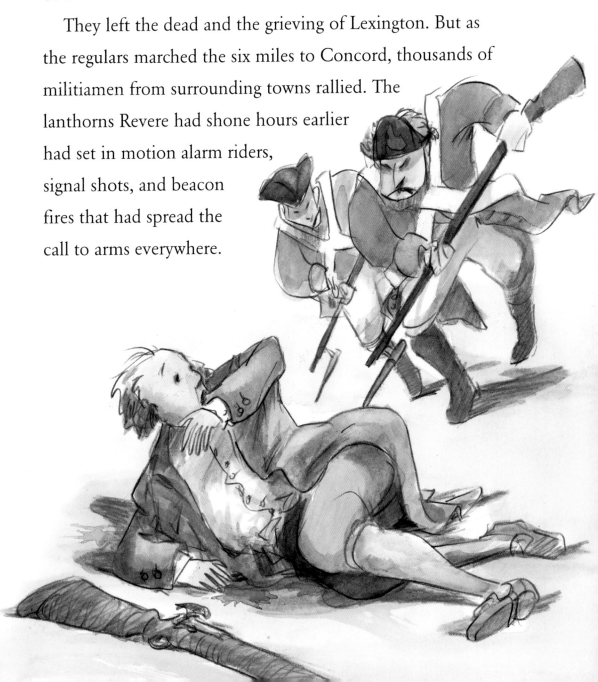

At 9 a.m., the regulars reached Concord. At first, the militiamen withdrew from the town to a low hill beside the narrow Concord River. Below them was the North Bridge.

About a hundred redcoats, a group splintered from the main body, lined up against them on the other side of the bridge.

In the town, Major Pitcairn led the search for powder and arms, discovering only a discouragingly small cache that included three cannons and wooden gun carriages. He disabled the guns and set the carriages afire. But as they burned, the flames leaped to the town's courthouse and it began to burn too. Despite their mutual distrust, the Yankees and redcoats joined together in a bucket brigade and doused the flames.

At North Bridge, volunteers swelled the militia's ranks until about five hundred were present. They saw smoke rise from Concord and feared the worst.

"Will you let them burn the town down?" one challenged militia colonel James Barrett.

The colonel's old coat, flapped hat, and leather apron stood
in shabby contrast to the splendid scarlet and gold uniforms of
the British officers. Despite his unmilitary appearance, no one
hesitated when the colonel ordered the men to load their
weapons. He added the warning "not to fire until the British
fired first."

A young fifer played a jaunty tune and they all went forward.

"They began to march . . . down upon us . . . in a very
military manner," a regular remarked.

The militia's military bearing and larger numbers astonished
the redcoats and they fell back.

Then, as at Lexington, a shot was fired. But this time there was no mystery. It came from a regular acting without orders. Two other redcoats joined in, then the entire front rank. Musket balls tore into the militia.

Isaac Davis, captain of the neighboring town of Acton's militia, fell dead, as did a comrade.

The young fifer and three others were wounded.

Still, the Yankees came on.

Finally, Major Buttrick of Concord yelled, "Fire, fellow soldiers, for God's sake fire!"

Muskets fired. Balls flew. Smoke billowed. Regulars fell: three dead and nine wounded.

"The weight of their fire was such that we was obliged to give way, then run," said British ensign Jeremy Lister.

Simple farmers, mechanics, and clerks had scattered the famed soldiers of the British army!

The regulars fled to Concord to join the main body of troops, the wounded hobbling after them. A local man, Ammi White, raced to an injured soldier on the road, splitting the redcoat's skull with a hatchet, to the horror of Yankees and British alike.

Vast numbers of Yankees gathered in the hills as Colonel Smith assembled his men and ordered them back to Boston, twenty miles away. It was about noon. Many of the Yankees and British had been armed and on the move for ten hours and more.

The redcoats started along the lane back toward Lexington. At Meriam's Corner, a crossroad along the redcoats' march, rebels formed a battle line. One joked, "Stand trim, boys, or the rascals will shoot your elbows off!"

The clash at Meriam's Corner left more than wounded elbows. "A great many lay dead and the road bloody," said Yankee Amos Barrett. Militiamen from twenty-three surrounding towns would eventually shed their blood in the battle.

The regulars continued down the lane. As they retreated,
the rebels "concluded to scatter and make use of the trees and
walls for to defend us, and attack them." At a skirmish at a
bend in the road that would be remembered as Bloody Curve,
thirty redcoats fell. And outside Lexington, Captain Parker
and his bloodied militiamen hid behind granite boulders and
blasted the regulars at close range, knocking Colonel Smith
from his horse with a thigh wound. The fight would be
remembered as Parker's Revenge.

The redcoats were ambushed again. This time, Major Pitcairn was unhorsed. He was shaken but not wounded. Five of his men weren't so lucky and were killed.

"Our ammunition began to fail, and [some] were so fatigued that they were scarce able to act," said a regular. "[It] made a great confusion. We began to run rather than retreat in order."

The militiamen, "maddened and beside themselves," followed the redcoats into Lexington. Utter British defeat was a whisker away.

Then "cannons began to play."

Militiaman Loammi Baldwin said, "A ball came through the Meeting House, near my head. I retreated . . . and lay and heard the balls in the air and saw them strike the ground."

It was the work of newly arrived British artillerymen.

Back in Boston, a worried General Gage had dispatched Brigadier Lord Percy and another group of regulars with orders to assist Smith. Reaching Lexington in late afternoon, Percy was shocked to discover himself rescuing the colonel.

A big-nosed, bony man from a family of great wealth and privilege, Percy was a cool leader. Using two cannons he'd dragged with him, he drove away the Yankees. Then he folded Smith's men in with his own, and prepared for a fight all the way back to Boston.

Skillfully using his cannons to keep the rebels at bay, Percy nonetheless worried he had too few cannonballs. Gage had had the same worry and had sent a small convoy with extra cannonballs after Percy. They never arrived.

The wagons were ambushed by old men led by David Lamson, who killed the lead horses and two regulars and sent the rest of the redcoats fleeing for their lives. They surrendered at the soonest opportunity – which turned out to be to an elderly woman named Mother Batherick, who then delivered her prisoners to the local militia. Some in Britain later wondered, "If one old Yankee woman can take six grenadiers, how many soldiers will it require to conquer America?"

William Heath, a Massachusetts general, arrived to lead the Yankees. Heath was not a professional soldier but a country squire who'd learned war from books. He proved a close reader.

He ringed the retreating British with militiamen and a circle of fire, and "helped . . . pull people together, advised the best use of terrain, moved units down on the British."

Percy had once thought the Yankees were "villains" who "talk much and do little." Now he decided that they had "men amongst them who know very well what they're about."

The fighting continued into Menotomy, today's Arlington. Yankees and regulars fought from house to house.

Seventy-eight-year-old Samuel Whittemore hid himself behind a stone wall and attacked the redcoats with a musket, two pistols, and a sword. He killed one and wounded another before half his face was shot away, and he was bayoneted fourteen times. But "Flinty Whittemore" survived the ghastly wounds and lived until age ninety-six.

Forty regulars and twenty-five Yankees died in Menotomy.

The British were nearly home, but the rebels had torn up the Charles River bridge that led to Boston, trapping the redcoats on the wrong bank. Cleverly, Percy abandoned the idea of reaching Boston and, instead, led his men to a hill in the waterside town of Charlestown.

Nearby lay the British warship *Somerset* and her roaring cannons. As the sun set, the ship's guns frightened away the Yankees. The regulars had finally reached safety. Among the last to escape was Major Pitcairn, a player in the very first fighting.

The road between Charlestown and Concord lay strewn with dead men and horses. Seventy-three redcoats died and 174 were wounded. The Yankees suffered 49 dead and 39 wounded.

The fight of April 19 proved to be "a hinge . . . on which a large future was to turn." The battle, said writer Thomas Paine, set "the country . . . on fire above my ears."

The stubborn Yankees finally forced England to accept American independence in 1783. Thousands died in the American Revolution, including headstrong Major Pitcairn, who died at the Battle of Bunker Hill.

Disease killed Captain Parker months after the fight on the village green.

Samuel Adams and John Hancock signed the Declaration of Independence. Each was also later governor of Massachusetts.

General Heath continued to use book-learned war skills in the Revolution, as did the man who sold him the books, Henry Knox.

Paul Revere took part in several battles of the war. Later, he enlarged his reputation as a great silversmith.

Colonel Smith fought without distinction but still managed to be promoted to general.

Percy fought well but resigned his command in disgust with the war. He became the richest man in England.

General Gage lost the Battle of Bunker Hill and retired to England. In 1787, eleven years after America's Declaration of Independence, Gage died, still holding the title royal governor of Massachusetts.

George III, the king who'd started his reign so well, ended badly. He passed his last years raving mad and chained to a chair.

# Bibliography

Bailyn, Bernard. *Faces of the Revolution*. New York: Knopf, 1990.

Bakeless, John. *Turncoats, Traitors, and Heroes*. Philadelphia: Lippincott, 1959.

Coburn, Frank. *The Battle of April 19, 1775*. Port Washington, N.Y.: Kennikat Press, 1912.

Fischer, David Hackett. *Paul Revere's Ride*. New York: Oxford University Press, 1994.

Gross, Robert. *The Minutemen and Their World*. New York: Hill & Wang, 1976.

Langgurth, A. J. *Patriots*. New York: Simon & Shuster, 1988.

Pearson, Michael. *Those Damned Rebels*. New York: Putnam's Sons, 1972.

Piper, Fred. *Lexington*. Lexington, Mass.: Lexington Historical Society, 1963.

Sabin, Douglas. *April 19, 1775: A Historiographic Study*. Concord, Mass.: National Park Service, 1987.